Book Coach – The Self-Publishing Maven
Cover Design – Okomota
Editing – Susan Andres and Robin Devonish
Interior Design – Inkcept Studio

ISBN – 978-1-7350056-0-7

www.CrystalGoliday.com

ACKNOWLEDGMENTS

I did not get to where I am by myself. I want to thank the *Village* that helped raise me, starting back to my ancestors, who endured a lot for future generations. While we may think life is hard today, it was even harder back then.

My parents worked their butts off to make sure I had what I needed, and I appreciate them for all the lessons I learned from them through their words and actions.

I am blessed with an extended family, which I affectionately call my Framily. I love them dearly and wish each one of them all the best.

My communities throughout the various phases of my life:

- O Co-op City, Bronx, NY
- O   Y.A.C. (Youth Activities Committee)
- O Middle School 181
- O Project ESTEEM
- O Monsignor Scanlan High School
- O Drexel University and everyone I interacted with during my time there
- O My second homes Philly, DC, Maryland and Virginia
- O Anyone who has ever said a prayer for me

I THANK YOU! Each one of you is appreciated. Know that there are more good things to come from me.

DEDICATION

I dedicate this book to my Parents, Husband, Prince, the communities that helped raise me, and the youth around the world.

O My Parents are now a part of my *Team of Angels* up in heaven. I am a product of their hard work and dedication, which I appreciate. I hope this book makes them proud, as this is their book too. I miss them dearly. I hope I continue to make them proud as I work daily to make a positive impact in this world.

- My Husband is my life partner. He supports and challenges my ideas—both of which help me to be a better me every day.

- My Prince provides me with a different outlook on life and renewed energy. I love having him around and am honored to be his Momma.

- The communities that helped raise me in New York City, Pennsylvania, and the DMV (DC, Maryland, and Virginia) area have taught me so much. This girl from Section 5 in Co-op City appreciates you and will continue to *lift as I climb*.

- The younger generation of the world is so inspiring and has so much potential. Allow the use of this book to help you be a positive asset in the world, believing in yourself.

INTRODUCTION

H ave you ever wanted to pursue a dream, but didn't have the funding to make it become a reality? Well, this book will provide you with steps to obtain funding for a college degree. With information broken down into actionable steps, this book will help your dream become a reality.

Both of my parents worked for prestigious companies and had a steady income, but other factors came into place that accounted for where their money went. From being in two different homes with a stack of bills and the increasing cost to attend college, I decided that I didn't want anyone or anything to deter me from advancing my education when the time came to attend college. Also, I didn't want to place another bill on my parents.

Between the ages of 11 to 14 years old, I realized there might be some limitations if I relied on their finances. The situation that highlighted this thought was when I decided to leave the New York City public school system after middle school. With being more aware of the increase of violence in the city with gangs to worrying about what to wear every day, I wanted a change. The change was going to a private catholic school for high school.

When looking back at the amount for high school tuition (which was about $300 a month), it may not seem like much today. However, it was another bill for my parents to pay. And while I know my parents would've sacrificed, I was listening to the arguments they had over the rent and then my tuition for high school in my freshman year. That one and several other discussions stuck with me so much that while in high school, I learned about a sponsorship program (where parents in that program were paying less than $50 a month meanwhile my parents were paying more than $300 a month) and other scholarship opportunities. The kicker was the amount of one of my parents' salaries was too much to qualify for the sponsorship program because it was based on your income, so I had to wait until my sophomore year to obtain any of the scholarships offered. That's when my journey began to go after scholarships to finish high school.

I not only received scholarships to attend Monsignor Scanlan High School, but my journey also resulted in a full-ride academic scholarship that paid for my tuition **and** housing to attend college. Also, I was awarded another scholarship for my time in college that covered my fees. Over time I learned that my more substantial scholarship was in partnership with the college I attended (Drexel University) and not just the funding from NACME (National Action Council for Minorities in Engineering) where I learned about the initial scholarship.

The award stipulation was the school paid 80%, and the organization paid 20% for my tuition **and** housing for the five-year co-op program.

I was in pursuit of a Bachelor of Science in Computer Engineering. I must add that the housing also covered off-campus housing, a nice touch when I became an upperclassman. Once I discovered this information, I found out all the details. Before you knew it, I had my first apartment paid for by my scholarship. It was an amazing feeling.

My journey of obtaining funding for college degrees did not stop there but expanded beyond my undergraduate years. I took a gap year to work full time, and then I decided to pursue graduate school. During this time, I discovered another funding source where companies paid for college degrees. I learned the qualifications necessary, which sometimes included maintaining a specific Grade Point Average (GPA), staying with a company for a particular length of time, and steps required for approval. For example, before taking the courses providing proof of your grades, bill, etc. I moved forward with pursuing not one but two graduate degrees (Master of Science in Technology Management and a Master of Business Administration). I even thought about the highest-level degree of Ph.D. but decided not to because I did not need it in the direction I wanted to go.

During my adult years, I realized that many people go into significant debt to get a college degree, and I know there is another and better way. In this book, I will share the funding sources that paid for my three college degrees and additional information I learned over the years. I know that families, for many generations, will benefit from this knowledge.

Now this book is not for you if you:

1. Do not want to advance your education.
2. Want things handed to you.

3. Are unwilling to do the work, as this requires research and taking action.
4. Looking for a student loan repayment plan.

If the above doesn't apply, I look forward to walking you through how to get a college degree for free. Let's start with the first chapter *"Why Me?"*

CONTENTS

Why Me? 15

Getting Started! 25

Who Has It? 37

What's Next? 57

Conclusion 63

*"Education is the key to unlocking the world,
a passport to freedom."*

— Oprah Winfrey

WHY ME?

*"Embrace what makes you unique,
even if it makes others uncomfortable.
I didn't have to become perfect because I've learned
throughout my journey that perfection is the
enemy of greatness."*

— **Janelle Monae**

When speaking with me today, most wouldn't know that I stuttered and read below the recommended grade level in my early elementary school years. Yes, I had issues that came to a head when I was in the first grade at my school named after Walt Disney in the Bronx, New York. It was a typical school day, and I vividly remember when my first-grade teacher (we'll call her Ms. S) was calling students to read out loud. I made sure not to make eye contact with her hoping she wouldn't call on me. But guess who Ms. S called on to read. Me!

Well, I struggled to read the assigned section; it took me a while to get words out, and then I said some of the words wrong. Instead of helping me and being compassionate in her response, Ms. S made a joke, then my classmates laughed. Now I can't remember exactly what she said, but the sting of my classmates laughing at me was embarrassing, and it hurt that a teacher would make me feel that way. It was not a characteristic you would think of when Disney comes to mind.

Thinking back, Ms. S was wrong for not using that moment to help me, it did not serve as a served as a teachable moment for the entire class. I'm sure there was another way she could've approached that situation. I mean, I was hurt so deep that I still remember the incident from decades ago. Now that I think about it, my developmental delay compounded along with the episode I just described may have attributed to me being very shy when I was younger. I would come into a room, and I would take a while to warm up. So, I kept to myself and remained quiet. Growing up in New York City, I learned to have a stone face quickly (a stern look or what some call a "game face," but to some you look mean), and with me being shy, I appeared unfriendly to some. Those who knew me understood that wasn't the case.

Due to my low reading and speech performance, I went to speech class and was excused from regular class activities to get specialized help. Looking back, I am not sure if it was my grades, Ms. S, or my dedicated Momma, who made that happen, **but** I am appreciative. Those sessions helped me to improve in reading and speech and taught me how to turn a negative situation into a positive one. My Momma also kept me busy seven days a week with programs provided by an organization called Y.A.C., Youth Activities Committee. One of the Y.A.C. programs that helped with my reading and literacy skills was their Saturday Tutorial Program. While many of my peers were at home watching cartoons or sleeping in, I was at the neighborhood Einstein Community Center getting tutored. I appreciate Y.A.C. so much that I recently started a nonprofit organization called *Never Underestimate Knowledge (NUK)*. The part of my journey where I received assistance illuminates the saying we've heard that is "Hard Work Pays Off."

Incremental improvement compounded over the years. I learned the studying techniques that worked for me. With math as my favorite subject, I reminded myself that I needed to read the text to see how the example problem was solved to understand how to move forward with the rest of the assignment. I did not get a 100 percent on literacy exams (even today, I prefer an audio book over sitting to read one), but I appreciate a book and all it feeds the mind and soul. I hope that my writing this book will do the same for so many others.

After learning what worked for me, I was placed in some advanced classes in junior high school, which went from fifth to eighth grades. It was called the "Exceptionally Gifted" (EG) program in a school named after Pablo Casals, the cellist. Two things I want to point out:

1. You had to test into the EG program, but I was ***handpicked*** midway through seventh grade—a reflection of the seeds people sowed in me throughout the years.

2. I enjoyed junior high school, from excelling academically and being more sociable to broadening my horizon by learning to play the viola.

By the time I reached high school, I was advanced in some subjects and placed in the honors track in my private Catholic school, which was their highest academic track. I was a member of all of what I like to call brainiac clubs, but I was a "cool nerd." (Fifteen years after I graduated, I returned and shared this with the graduating class, so they know it is *ok* to be intelligent; you can still be cool.) I made the step team in my freshman year, which was the "it" extracurricular activity, and by senior year, I was asked to be the captain (which I declined because I wanted to focus on other things that year).

When it came time for my high school graduation, I was not the valedictorian or the salutatorian. *Still*, I received the *most* awards, had a speaking part, and had *full* financial support to pay for my undergraduate studies in Computer

Engineering at Drexel University in what would be my new home—Philadelphia, Pennsylvania (Philly).

To top it off, the full financial support I received came from one significant academic scholarship that paid for my housing **and** tuition provided by NACME (National Action Council for Minorities in Engineering) and a supplemental award that paid for my fees and books from ACE (opportunities in Architecture, Construction, and Engineering). With these blessings, which I see as the fruits of my labor and those who supported me, several families of my fellow graduates congratulated me after the ceremony. My high school graduation opened my eyes to see that anything is possible. From all the things I mentioned to you, I am still on cloud nine from my high school graduation. I am in continual gratitude to two of my **angels** in heaven—my parents.

My parents **worked**, and they had **bills** to pay. So, even though I had the Reebok Freestyle Hi sneaker (the "54.11s") in almost every color, my parents were not rich, and I'm happy I did not have to put another bill on them to pay for my college education. Funding a college education is more than just tuition. If you do the math for all expenses (the cost of laundry, toiletries, travel, and so on), the price tag for college keeps rising.

If I had the contact information for Ms. S., my first-grade teacher, she would be the person I would eagerly keep informed of my accomplishments. Some of which are being recruited and relocated right after college to work for Lockheed Martin (a Fortune 500 company), the international publications about me that were made by Accenture (Fortune Magazine world's most admired Information Technology Services company that I worked for more than a decade), many public-speaking engagements, the awards I've won for both my academics and leadership, my life accomplishments, and the three degrees I earned free because organizations and companies believed in me. I'm unsure of what her intentions were when she was my teacher or whether she would even remember me, but what I would want her to get out of my update would be to sow seeds in our youth, not hinder them with negativity.

I want us **all** to **win** and know there is an opportunity out there for everyone. We must find the opportunity and go after it. The ones who put in the work will reap the benefits (and let's face it, sometimes people have the stars aligned in their favor some way). Have you heard the sayings "what is meant for you is for you" or "you reap what you sow"? Well, I am a living manifestation of those sayings. If a young lady from Co-op City in the Bronx who struggled with her reading and speech could be successful and have all three of her college degrees paid for, then **why not you**?

It is time to **believe** in yourself and **put in the work** to turn your **dreams** into **reality**! You are deserving, and it's your time. You took the first step by getting this book. Now, I will show you how to get to the point of earning your degrees for free.

GETTING STARTED!

"Learning that sometimes people come into our lives, not to GIVE us what we need, but to TEACH us what we need.

—Tiffany "The Budgetnista" Aliche

Every child is asked the question, "What do you want to be when you grow up?" at least once. Looking back, it might annoy us to think of how many times we were asked that question. Well, this is a starting point to determine the path you will take to become whatever your answer is to that question, in addition to ultimately get funding to pursue it. When I was growing up, my response was, "I want to be a singer (thinking I would one day hit the notes like Whitney Houston), an actress (like my sorority sister Phylicia Rashad), and a lawyer (just like the character of Clair Huxtable on *The Cosby Show*)." But over time, my answer changed.

Through life experiences, I realized that I am not a singer (except in my dreams or the shower), and my passion was not in acting or being a lawyer. So, I want you to use this question as a self-reflecting tool at different stages in your life so you can think about where you want to be in the future and which educational path you need to pursue. A good timetable to ask this question is during the different levels of school. For example, my answer in elementary and middle school differed from my reply in high school.

Answering this question is a critical factor in obtaining the most funding because the criteria for some scholarships could be specific, down to studying in a particular field (i.e.-scholarship for someone who wants to pursue a degree in Computer Engineering opposed to just Engineering, which is a broader discipline).

At a young age, I didn't imagine that I would study engineering and business, earn my degrees in these fields, then become a corporate executive in a Fortune 500 company and passionate philanthropist advocating for our youth (with a focus on inner-city youth) and women (particularly domestic violence survivors). Through my life experiences, I realized my destination stemmed from my interest in math and having my mother as a chaperone or volunteer for many activities in which I participated.

It also originated from being victimized by someone I knew in a violent domestic relationship, which prayerfully I got out of and had the support of others (both those I knew and others I did not know through city workers such as the police department and my legal team and the nonprofit organization that worked with me during this horrific period) to move forward in life. This led to my desire to provide resources to inner-city youth and domestic violence survivors then starting my nonprofit organization, *Never Underestimate Knowledge* (NUK) in 2019. My goals came from asking myself, *"What do I want to be when I grow up?"* And yes, I still ask myself that question and others.

I focused on my answer to this question near the end of my time in high school. We all know that junior year in high school is a crucial year to prepare for college, from taking essential exams such as the SAT to using junior year grades to determine what we put on our college applications. So, my answer to the question, *"What do I want to be when I grow up?"* was even then unclear. I dug deeper internally to ask myself, *"Which subjects do I like?"* The subject that came out on top was math, and I had a strong interest in science.

From there, I searched for jobs with a great deal of math. The ones that came up were accountant, engineer, and stockbroker. These titles leave room for interpretation, so I further researched them to see what they mean. Through my research at my school career services office, the public library, and on the computer, I discovered that being an accountant and stockbroker involved mainly math, but engineering had a good combination of math and science.

Through my research, I also found that there were many disciplines within engineering (chemical, civil, computer, electrical, industrial, mechanical, and so on) that I could explore. Knowing this was a great starting point to search funding sources to make my college experience free for me and one less bill for my parents.

The question of *"What do I want to be when I grow up?"* and other questions such as:

- What makes me happy?
- What do I like to do?
- How could I turn my passion into a career?
- What does it take to make all this happen?

should be questions you ask yourself. And know that it's OK if you don't know the exact answer to them all. As you see from my taking you back through my eleventh-grade mindset, I had to dig a little deeper with the first question of "What do I want to be when I grow up?" because I did not know the exact answer to it myself.

To get the full picture of which subject you want to pursue for your college degree and what it takes to get there, you need to use the Internet and your network. Don't be afraid to tap into other people's networks and ask the people you know to refer someone to you in your field of interest. Over the years, I met many people. I've told my Framily (the term I use for my family and friends) that if I don't know the answer to their question, I'm sure I can find someone who does because I have a **powerful** network.

I want you to research the field of study you wish to pursue:

○ Understand what that field entails to earn that degree and succeed.

▷ From my research, engineering required many math and science courses for the first several years. Then the remaining years required classes in the discipline (chemical, civil, computer, electrical, mechanical, and so on). There were also opportunities for electives (courses related or unrelated to the major).

O Learn what an everyday routine is like in that field.

   ▷ The discipline (which path in engineering) determined what an everyday routine looked like. After asking the college advisor which engineering discipline had the most math, I knew I wanted to pursue computer engineering. I learned that a computer engineer could spend their day behind a computer coding or in a lab working on a computer's hardware.

O Understand the options on how to pursue it, including the pros and cons.

   ▷ I learned that with an engineering degree, the starting salary is high, and there are options to go deeper into the field (an advanced degree, which depends on how technical you want to get into it).

▷ Some positive attributes (pros) to pursuing engineering are it teaches you analytical thinking and opens the door to many other fields. Several people I studied engineering with decided to become lawyers, dentists, and other professions.

▷ Some negative or not so favorable attributes to pursuing engineering as a field of study are that you have less time to socialize in college because it is an intensive major. You are required to prove your expertise in more ways than other fields (in a lecture, lab, recitation, major presentations, and so on).

○ Learn from the journey of others.

▷ While in high school, I participated in a program at Manhattan College. The summer was all about engineering. During that time, I spoke to those who worked there to learn about what they did to get to where they are and got their opinion on whether they recommended that path and why.

The key here is to learn from what other people experienced. You don't want to duplicate their every step, but it helps you to decide what you want to adapt for your journey and what you want to leave because it doesn't fit in your life.

I will help you walk through your journey of finding funding to pursue your dreams. Let's move on to the topic of where you can find the money.

"You can't just sit there and wait for people to give you that golden dream. You've got to get out there and make it happen for yourself."

— Diana Ross

WHO
HAS IT?

"I'd rather regret the risks that didn't work out than the chances I didn't take at all."

— **Simone Biles**

Money is all around us! Did you know that? From corporations to foundations to individuals, there are forms of money out there for you. You might wonder where to start. Let's discuss different types of money that are available:

- O Grants
- O Scholarships
- O Student Loans

In this book, I focus on scholarships, as I know this firsthand. However, it is good to know other common sources of funding. Grants are other sources of funding that do **not** require repayment. However, student loans must be paid back after graduation. Grants and scholarships are better ways to pay for college, so focus your search on those funding sources.

My Journey

My journey was funded by scholarships for my undergrad—one large academic one from NACME that paid for my **full** tuition and housing and another from ACE. Two companies (Lockheed Martin and Accenture) paid for my graduate degrees (Master of Science in Technology Management and Master of Business Administration). There were varying paths to obtain the funding for my three degrees, so understand that each source of funding may require different qualifications.

I started my scholarship search between my junior and senior years of high school by investing in *The Scholarship Book*. This book was thick, like one of the textbooks I had for my high school classes or an encyclopedia. It had many scholarships listed in it and included information such as the name, description, amount awarded, and the due date for each scholarship. This was the real start of my search to find funding for college.

I wrote a letter to those scholarships I was interested in to learn more about them. Every place should have someone on the other end eagerly waiting to write you back, but that was not always the case. The response rate of returned detailed response letters was less than I expected. However, I did not give up. My mother and I tapped into our networks to learn more about other opportunities. I recently told a group of high schoolers that your **network is your net worth**. What I'm about to explain to you is a testament to that statement.

After discussing my plans to go to college with my family and expressing my interest in studying engineering, my late aunt told me about an organization called NACME. By this time, I was in my senior year of high school. The application was due in the first quarter of the calendar year. I answered the questions and provided my essay, so they knew more about me, and I waited for a response.

After some time, I was invited in for an interview, which I passed. I was then invited to a mathematical assessment which was a way for them to see how I interacted with my peers to solve complex problems. (Think back to a pro I mentioned about studying engineering in the prior chapter, and you will understand why they had this intricate component, which I did not fully understand back then).

I thought maybe they were doing it to see how smart I was, but looking back, if I were investing a great deal of money into people, I would want to get to know them beyond just what they submitted in an application. Drexel University was the first school to let me know I was accepted. I received that letter in March during my senior year in high school. Now that I have my nonprofit that focuses on providing resources such as scholarships to inner-city youth, I should probably do a case study on them to learn more about their process because that offering was awesome and helped so many families. But wait, there's more.

After discovering that I received the scholarship later in my senior year, I was notified that I would be provided an all-expenses-paid trip to Texas A&M University for their Summer Immersion Program. During this program, they prepared me for the worst professor. This was yet another great perk of this scholarship. I did not have to pay a dime. NACME paid for my travel, housing in a college dorm, and food.

This was such a cool opportunity to meet other people awarded the same scholarship from around the nation. I also met my first college roommate from this process, who is now one of my best friends. She was also one of my maids of honor at my wedding (I had two) and godmother to my Prince. These experiences, along with a Winter Immersion I attended for several years, made me realize how blessed I was and reconfirmed that hard work pays off.

During my college years, I spoke to scholars younger than I. I knew then that I wanted to share my experience with others, but I waited decades later to start my nonprofit and write this book. I am happy I finally sat down to write this book and share this topic with you. It's just sad that it took both of my parents to pass away for me to take these steps. Nonetheless, I am making it happen and want to remove any financial stress from families through my efforts.

Now my funding for my undergraduate studies did not stop there. During the summer between my junior and senior years of high school, I attended a program at Manhattan College for students interested in engineering. We had classes and projects to complete during that timeframe, but it was also fun.

From there, I was invited to attend ACE during my senior year. This program broke down the large cohort of students into smaller groups paired with one university and a conglomerate of New York City companies in those three fields. At the end of the program, my group built a community manually, by drawing it, and electronically, in a program called AutoCAD. We were split into teams of two, and we focused on one house in the community. It was fun and an opportunity for me to think beyond the apartments and co-ops I was used to in the city.

As the program ended, graduating seniors were identified and informed about their scholarship opportunities. I happily applied to it and received it. The ACE scholarship was $500 a year. Although some might turn their nose up at hearing the amount, I was happy about it because college is more than just tuition and housing. There are also books (which are high-priced, and it seems like every semester there are new editions, so they have limited use), fees, board (which is for a meal plan), and more. So, my ACE scholarship came in handy.

NACME looked for someone in good academic standing; not everyone was a straight-A student. They also looked at community service involvement, your conduct in the interview, and with your peers (remember the assessments I mentioned) and a GPA at or above 2.5. To keep my ACE scholarship, I had to report my good academic standing to them (submit my transcript annually), and I received the money.

An executive with ACE was happy to receive my information because many of those who started with me did not come back for the remaining money they awarded. I remember in one conversation that I joked and told them they could send me more money. Although they seemed as though the organization would entertain my request, I quickly let them know I was joking. I didn't need the extra funding because I had the NACME Vanguard scholarship, and they could use the money for another student who needed it.

In retrospect, I wonder if that was a test to see whether I was greedy. Well, I passed that test, and more doors opened for me. I graduated from Drexel's five-year program with my Bachelor of Science in Computer Engineering on time with some co-op experience (a longer internship for six months and you get the salary for that field). And, I was recruited to work at what was one of the most sought-after companies, Lockheed Martin.

I find it funny that they always had the longest lines at career fairs, and I wouldn't get in them. But they found my resume online, flew me to DC for an interview, and provided hotel accommodations. Two days after my interview, while in Las Vegas with my Father, I learned I got the job. I had a conversation with my Daddy, who told me that he worked all his life for my starting salary. Hearing this reminded me that what was happening to me was also about my parents and the dedication they provided to me to be successful; so, I accepted the job offer.

After taking a gap year, which is a year between college studies, I pursued the next level. I worked and knew the job I had was not "where I wanted to be when I grew up" (you see how this question resurfaces), so I decided to research graduate schools.

From using my network and learning the offerings and their associated policies, I discovered that the company I worked for had a program that pays for you to pursue a degree. You had to earn a certain grade in the class, and this company paid for tuition and books. I researched other places, and one of my former Lockheed Martin colleagues who worked for one of the government agencies told me the details of the program there. That agency paid for tuition and books, and you did not have to work while you pursued your degree, but you owed the agency two years of service after completing your studies.

You see, there are pros and cons to every situation. So, please always weigh your options, and don't dive into the first thing presented to you. Do your research, and do what's best for you! Looking back, two years was not much time. However, at the time, it seemed like forever.

I stayed with Lockheed for a few years, and then continued my career elsewhere. That ended their funding for my graduate degree. And remember that I decided to pursue two graduate degrees while working full time.

But fortunately for me, the next company that recruited me (Accenture) had a different program I used to continue funding my graduate college degrees. With them, I needed to use my annual training budget and explain how the classes related to my career path and goals. I happily did that and received the funding. It did not cover my books, but that was OK with me.

In hindsight, I found the graduate school funding process required more in the application process. Maybe I felt that way because, in high school, I was in the mode of continual schoolwork. Therefore, the scholarship application process did not seem like a lot of work. Also, my amazingly resourceful Mommy was in my corner to help get things done. Regardless, for both companies, I had to explain why they should fund my specific courses. Now I understand it was an additional investment they were making in me on top of the nice salary I received.

Your Journey

Even beyond my experience, I've heard about other avenues for you to explore. As I talked to those in my network about my book idea, I discovered other forms of funding, aside from scholarships that I want to bring to your attention. They are grants and alumni funding sources.

Although I found that scholarships were paid to the school or as a check to me to pay for it, grants seem similar. When speaking more about grants, one of my accountability partners used her grant money for things such as books. While we're on the topic of books, let me share some sources to eliminate or at least minimize that cost that can add up:

- Ask upper-level students to borrow or purchase their book. I promise you it would be cheaper than buying a new one. Also, if the edition changed, it is usually from minor edits, or a chapter added. You could always work with your classmates or professor to align the topics in the older version.

O Use the school and public libraries. Over the years, I've seen less use of the library, but don't sleep on it . . . it's a gold mine in there!

A source new to me is alumni funding. This is something along the lines of a "home" scholarship, where an alumni group in a particular area (say Washington, DC) who attended Dillard University (in New Orleans) provides a student from Washington, DC a scholarship to attend Dillard University. "How do I find out about that?" I was told to look on the alumni pages of the schools to see what's offered.

Know that to find this money, you will have to do the legwork. Some apps help you find them, but remember you have to also organize your search with:

O keywords
O your interest (i.e.- engineering)

- locations in which you're interested in attending college

With technology, information is at your fingertips. Don't forget to use your network. As the saying goes, "*a closed mouth don't get fed*." Besides the popular sources, there might be some undiscovered sources into which you could tap. For example, I started my nonprofit *Never Underestimate Knowledge* (NUK) in 2019, and my goal is to have a scholarship designated for various states in addition to providing resources to inner-city youth and domestic violence survivors.

To give you examples, I researched the top five college majors in 2019:

- Business
- Communications
- Criminal Justice
- Nursing
- Psychology

If you are interested in these fields, then you're in luck because I did some research to provide you with three sources that range in the amount awarded and submission dates, but most are $5,000 or more. Regardless of the major you pursue, sites such as www.scholarships.com and the Scholly platform at www.myscholly.com are dedicated to providing scholarship resources at your fingertips. So, use them for your search.

Here are scholarships in the 2019 popular majors to get you started:

O Business

   ▷ Hyundai Scholarship awards $20,000, and the submission deadline is March 5.

   ▷ Jane M. Klausman Women in Business Scholarship awards $8,000, and the submission deadline varies.

- ▷ David R. Parsley Scholarship Fund for Supply Chain Management awards $10,000, and the submission deadline is March 15.

- O Communications

  - ▷ BMI Founders Award for Radio Broadcasting awards $5,000, and the submission deadline is February 1.
  - ▷ Mercatus Adam Smith Fellowship awards $10,000, and the submission deadline is March 15.
  - ▷ Ray Greenly Scholarship awards $25,000, and the submission deadline is April 3.

- O Criminal Justice

  - ▷ Ritchie-Jennings Memorial Scholarship awards $10,000, and the submission deadline is January 30.

- ▷ Ruth D. Peterson Fellowship for Racial and Ethnic Diversity awards $6,000, and the submission deadline is March 1.
- ▷ ISF (Islamic Scholarship Fund) National Scholarship awards $5,000, and the submission deadline is March 21.

O Nursing

- ▷ Perinatal Graduate Nursing Scholarship awards $5,000, and the submission deadline is January 31.
- ▷ Gladys Carol Scholarship awards $5,000, and the submission deadline is March 31.
- ▷ National Black Nurses Association (NBNA) Scholarship awards $6,000, and the submission deadline is April 15.

○ Psychology

▷ Catching the Dream Program awards $5,000, and the submission deadline varies.

▷ Clarkston Scholars Program awards $10,000, and the submission deadline is January 15.

▷ College of Saint Rose Academic Scholarship awards $22,000, and the submission deadline is February 15.

To stay on top of the resources you find, you must keep track of everything. In the next chapter, I share some tips on how to do that. Before I do that, one parting thing I want you to keep in mind from this chapter is to **reach out** to the companies (specific points of contact identified for a particular department if you're already working for a company or general emails you see on websites), people you know, your mentors, and even post about your search on your social media platforms. You never know where you might discover information about funding sources.

WHAT'S NEXT?

*"In complete darkness we are all the same;
it is only our knowledge and wisdom that separates
us. Don't let your eyes deceive you."*

— Janet Jackson

To keep track of all information from funding sources (scholarships, alumni, grants, and so on) you receive, identify the software that you like to document it all in one place. I found a spreadsheet format that worked best for me, so I recommend programs such as Microsoft's Excel and Google's Sheets. Additionally, a free app called Quip allows you to use their interactive "Live Apps" features to assign tasks, communicate status, check off items, and link related documents.

And if you're a pen and paper person, don't worry. You could do the same that way, but it might be a little challenging to update as you receive more information. Regardless, do what works best for you.

In your spreadsheet, you should document pertinent information regarding what's required to obtain and keep it. Here are is a list of topics to get you started:

- Organization name
- Scholarship details
- Qualifying criteria
- Deadline to apply
- What needs to be submitted
- Award date
- Scholarship amount
- Requirements to keep the scholarship (especially for multiyear funding sources)

Here is an example of what your spreadsheet could look like. Please see the resources section of the book for a full spreadsheet to use.

#	Organization name	Scholarship details	Qualifying criteria	Deadline to apply	What needs to be submitted	Award date	Scholarship amount	Requirements to keep the scholarship (if multiyear)
1	Example Organization	Recognizes and rewards outstanding student achievement.	Attend a college/ university 3.0 GPA or higher	March 31st	Completed application Letter of recommend Essay Transcript	May 1st	$25,000 every year	Mail transcript after every semester
2								
3								
4								
5								

If you need any help with this or want to use any tools and services I provide, visit me at www.CrystalGoliday.com today.

Note that it is helpful to have an essay ready about you, which includes your accomplishments and goals. This essay could be used to answer the questions required in the application process. Note that there might be different questions asked, but your essay is a good starting point and could be attached even if it is not required. Look at it as a way for the organization to get to know you better.

Now that you know what information to collect, gather the necessary information, and keep track of the dates. You need to be organized throughout this process because you don't want to miss deadlines. Another thing I learned from being on both sides of the fence of receiving funds and administering funds is that even if you don't meet all criteria, do not be discouraged. ***Still apply*** because there is money out there, and organizations have it allocated for this purpose.

CONCLUSION

"Everything is worth it.
The hard work, the times when you're tired,
the times where you're a bit sad, in the end, it's all
worth it because it really makes me happy.
There's nothing better than loving
what you do."

— Aaliyah

n my journey, three things helped me get my three degrees free:

1. My desire to want more for myself and not burden my parents, who both worked hard and instilled in me to go to school (including college) -> work for a good company -> retire. Let's put a pin right here and I will come back to this point.

2. *The Scholarship Book* I used, but now you have everything at your fingertips through the Internet.

3. My network, which is super helpful for me and many others. I must say I know some pretty cool and knowledgeable people from various aspects of my life. One huge contributor to this aspect of my life was my maternal aunt. She knew about the

organization (NACME) that invested in me with their Vanguard scholarship. The organization paid my **full** tuition **and** housing for my five years in the Co-op Program at Drexel University for my Bachelor of Science degree in Computer Engineering.

The point of my telling you all this is for you to **use your resources**. Information is all around you. Open your mouth and express your goals. Know your yes could be in the room, and remember that the worst someone could say is no. And even if they say no, they know your request and could keep you in mind if information presents itself to them.

In this book, I told you about my journey from elementary school, my being able to pursue three degrees and have them all paid for, to now working full time and having my companies that include my living out my life passion with my nonprofit organization *Never Underestimate Knowledge* (NUK). Then, I took you through self-reflecting questions you have to ask yourself periodically to make sure you're on track to achieve the goal of what you want to be when you grow up. There, I outlined detailed steps for you to dig deeper to understand whether your thinking aligns with what happens in that field. Furthermore, you could learn from other people's mistakes along the way.

I kicked off the "money chapter" Who Has It? this informed you of different ways you could obtain money and narrowed in on my expertise of **scholarships**. But I did not stop there. I identified the top five college majors to get you started with a list of scholarships. Also, you have the start of your spreadsheet to document your scholarships and recommended software programs you could use to keep track of them.

Make sure you keep track of deadlines, follow up to confirm receipt of your application, ask how the award announcement will be administered, and make sure you have the date. Track the decisions in your spreadsheet (create a column for it if you don't already have one) and remember to **celebrate**!

I look forward to hearing about the funding you receive so you, too, can earn your college degree free. Be sure to keep in contact with me on the various social media platforms (Facebook, Instagram, LinkedIn, etc.) and head over to www. CrystalGoliday.com to sign up for my mailing list to stay updated on the products and services I offer.

IMPORTANT QUESTIONS AND RESOURCES

Answer the questions below to help you to create a blueprint for your future.

My favorite subjects in school are? ....

....

....

....

....

....

....

....

....

....

....

....

....

....

....

....

....

....

....

....

....

Which professions require the most use of these subjects?......

....

....

....

....

....

....

....

....

....

....

....

....

....

....

....

What do I like to do? ....

....

....

....

....

....

....

....

....

....

....

....

....

....

....

What do I want to be when I get older? ....

....

....

....

....

....

....

....

....

....

....

....

....

....

....

....

What am I passionate about and how can I turn it into a
career? ....

....

....

....

....

....

....

....

....

....

....

....

....

....

What will it take to make things happen? Do I need a degree
to pursue my passion? ....

....

....

....

....

....

....

....

....

....

....

....

....

....

....

....

....

....

....

What major(s) am I interested in pursuing in college? ....

....

....

....

....

....

....

....

....

....

....

....

....

....

....

Which locations (state, city, town, etc.) would I like to live? ...

....

....

....

....

....

....

....

....

....

....

....

....

....

....

....

What is required for me to earn a degree in my field of interest and be successful? ....

....

....

....

....

....

....

....

....

....

....

....

....

....

What does a daily routine look like in that field? ....

....

....

....

....

....

....

....

....

....

....

....

....

....

....

....

What are the pros and cons of pursuing this field? ....

....

....

....

....

....

....

....

....

....

....

....

....

....

....

Who could mentor me in this field?..

....

....

....

....

....

....

....

....

....

....

....

....

....

....

What professional organizations are in this field? ....

....

....

....

....

....

....

....

....

....

....

....

....

....

....

....

ADDITIONAL SCHOLARSHIP RESOURCES

Books

- 101 Scholarship Applications (Revised 2020 Edition): What It Takes to Obtain a Debt-Free College Education
- College Scholarships 2020: The 5-Step Process & 10 Top Places To Find Billions In Scholarships
- College Scholarships for High School Students (grades 9-12)
- Confessions of a Scholarship Winner: The Secrets That Helped Me Win $500,000 in Free Money for College-How You Can Too!

- Financial Aid Handbook, Revised Edition: Getting the Education You Want for the Price You Can Afford
- How to Win College Scholarships: A Guide for Parents in 10 Easy Steps: 2020 4th Edition
- How to Write a Winning Scholarship Essay: 30 Essays That Won Over $3 Million in Scholarships
- LAUNCH: How to Get Your Kids Through College Debt-Free and Into Jobs They Love Afterward
- Pace Scholarship Academy's Ultimate National Scholarship Book: Designed for Middle and High School Students
- Paying for College, 2020 Edition: Everything You Need to Maximize Financial Aid and Afford College
- Scholarship Application Guide: Mega Scholarships
- Scholarships, Grants & Prizes
- Scholarship Strategies: Finding and Winning the Money You Need
- Senior Year Head Start: for 9th, 10th, and 11th Grade
- The Best 385 Colleges, 2020 Edition: In-Depth Profiles & Ranking Lists to Help Find the Right College For You (College Admissions Guides)

- The Best Value Colleges, 13th Edition: 75 Schools That Give You the Most for Your Money
- The HomeScholar Guide to College Admission and Scholarships: Homeschool Secrets to Getting Ready, Getting In and Getting Paid
- The Scholarship & Financial Aid Solution How to Go to College for Next to Nothing with Short Cuts, Tricks, and Tips from Start to Finish
- The Ultimate Scholarship Book 2020: Billions of Dollars in Scholarships, Grants and Prizes
- Winning Scholarships for College: An Insider's Guide to Paying for College

Websites

- https://www.acementor.org/students.scholarships/
- https://bigfuture.collegeboard.org/scholarship-search
- https://www.careeronestop.org/Toolkit/Training/find-scholarships.aspx

- https://www.collegexpress.com/scholarships/search
- http://www.collegescholarships.org/scholarships/
- https://www.debt.org/students/scholarships-and-grants/
- https://www.discover.com/student-loans/college-planning/scholarships/search
- https://www.fastweb.com/
- https://finaid.org/scholarships/
- https://myscholly.com/
- https://money.howstuffworks.com/personal-finance/college-planning/financial-aid/scholarship.htm
- https://www.nacme.org/
- https://www.niche.com/colleges/scholarships/
- http://www.oas.org/en/scholarships/
- https://www.petersons.com/scholarship-search.aspx
- https://www.salliemae.com/college-planning/tools/scholarship-search/
- https://scholarshipamerica.org/
- https://scholarships.uncf.org/Program/Search

- http://www.scholarshipmonkey.com/
- https://studentaid.gov/understand-aid/types/scholarships
- https://www.studiesabroad.com/admissions/funding-your-program/scholarships-and-grants
- https://superscholar.org/scholarships/25-popular-college-scholarships/

Track Your Scholarships

#	Organization name	Scholarship Details	Qualifying criteria	Deadline to apply	What needs to be submitted	Award date	Scholarship amount	Requirements to keep the scholarship (if multiyear)	Scholarship received (Yes / No)
	Example Organization	Recognizes and rewards outstanding student achievement	* Attend a college/ university * 3.0 GPA or higher	March	*Completed application * Letter of recommendation * Essay * Transcript	May	$25,000 per year	Mail transcript after every semester	
1									
2									
3									
4									
5									
6									
7									
8									
9									
10									
11									
12									
13									
14									
15									
16									
17									
18									
19									
20									